CHARLIE WAITE'S
ITALIAN LANDSCAPES

NEAR PELAGIO, EAST OF FLORENCE, TUSCANY

CHARLIE WAITE'S
ITALIAN LANDSCAPES

TEXT BY JOHN JULIUS NORWICH

HAMISH HAMILTON · LONDON

HAMISH HAMILTON LTD

Published by the Penguin Group
27 Wrights Lane, London W8 5TZ, England
Viking Penguin Inc., 40 West 23rd Street, New York, New York 10010, USA
Penguin Books Australia Ltd, Ringwood, Victoria, Australia
Penguin Books Canada Ltd, 2801 John Street, Markham, Ontario, Canada L3R 1B4
Penguin Books (NZ) Ltd, 182–190 Wairau Road, Auckland 10, New Zealand

Penguin Books Ltd, Registered Offices: Harmondsworth, Middlesex, England

First Published 1990
Copyright © Charlie Waite 1990
Copyright © in the introduction John Julius Norwich 1990

CIP data for this book is available from the British Library

Library of Congress Catalog Card Number: 89-82574

ISBN 0-241-12534-0

Printed in Singapore

The following illustrations appear in the text: South of Norcia, Umbria (p.6). Bellino, south of Cortina, Dolomites (p.7). West of
Fabriche, Tuscany (p.10). South west of Asciano, Tuscany (p.12). Mount Etna, Sicily (p.19). Castelmenardo, north of Avezzano
Abruzzi (p.22). Tuscany (p.24).

Acknowledgements: I would like to thank
Caroline Taggart for her constant encouragement and enthusiasm
and Peter Campbell for his excellent design. CW

FOR MY DAUGHTER, ELLA BAHAMA WHITE

SOUTH OF NORICIA, UMBRIA

ITALIAN LANDSCAPES

For some two thousand years Italy has been, to the peoples of northern Europe, both a dream and an objective. Over the centuries, however, the reasons for its attraction have, not surprisingly, changed. Throughout the middle ages and up to perhaps 1500 or thereabouts, the vast majority of those who dragged themselves across the Alps were pilgrims, all of them with but a single objective: the saving of their immortal souls. Their primary goal was almost invariably Rome, where they intended to pray at the shrines of both St Peter and St Paul; but their journey might well include, for good measure, those of St Matthew at Salerno, of St Mark in Venice and, quite possibly, of the Archangel Michael in his deep cave beneath Monte Gargano on the Adriatic Coast. They travelled hard, on horseback and on foot, and during the two or three years that they might expect to be on the road they must have had plenty of time to look about them; but of all the many accounts that they left behind, few if any give more than a cursory mention of the countryside through which they passed.

By the early sixteenth century, however, the pattern had begun to change. For some time the pilgrim traffic had been declining; and the Reformation, coming as it did hot on the heels of the new humanism, dealt it a further blow from which it was never fully to recover. Trade, on the other hand, was everywhere on the increase. It was, of course, nothing new to the peninsula: indeed, the great commercial city-republics of Genoa, Pisa and Venice were all well past their prime. But for the emerging nations of the north the attractions of commerce were becoming ever stronger; and it was above all the merchants who now thronged the execrable roads – or, whenever possible, the far more comfortable waterways – of Italy.

Now, too, there began to appear two more classes of traveller unknown in earlier centuries. The first was that of the professional diplomatist, a new career that was becoming increasingly fashionable among ambitious young noblemen. It was these who were perhaps chiefly responsible for bringing back the books which – together with the stories and travellers' tales that they had picked up on their way – made Italy, to the average Englishman of the late sixteenth century and early seventeenth centuries, the most exciting, romantic, passionate, vicious and thoroughly amoral country in the world; but of outward beauty, or even the outward appearance, of that country little or nothing was ever said or written. Is it not curious – to take but one example – that Shakespeare, neither in the first act of *Othello* or in any of the five acts of *The Merchant of Venice*, never once suggests that he even knows the single most interesting fact about that city – that it is built on the water and that, as Robert Browning put it, 'the sea's a street there'? We are forced to conclude that landscape was in those days something that was simply taken for granted; it possessed no inherent interest of its own. Those young noblemen, too, must have found the journeys long, and time lying heavy on their hands; but there is no evidence that for all their education they, any more than their merchant contemporaries or their pilgrim predecessors, spent any of it admiring the view.

The second category of modern travellers was infinitesimally small compared to the others and would have been laughed to scorn by the lot of them. It consisted of the few – the very few – who travelled for pleasure: men like the extraordinary Thomas Coryate, who between May and September 1608 walked nearly two thousand miles to Venice and back, visiting forty-five cities *en route* – an exhausting enough journey, one would have thought, the very memory of which persuaded him to hang up the pair of shoes that had done him such sterling service in the sanctuary of his parish church at Odcombe in Somerset, where they were to remain for well over a century until they crumbled into dust. Four years later he set off again, this time penetrating as far as India – from which, I regret to record, he never returned, dying in Agra in 1616, at the age of forty. The book that he left behind him, which he engagingly entitled his *Crudities*, remains for me one of the most entertaining travel books ever written; by his contemporaries, however, he was generally considered more than a little dotty – and they may well have been right.

Dotty or not Coryate was a pioneer; and in the hundred years following his death the trickle of travellers-for-pleasure became, if not the torrent that we know today, at least an ever-increasing flow. The age of the Grand Tour had come at last, and for nearly all Grand Tourists Italy was not only the final objective but the climax of their journey. At last, too, people were beginning to take an interest in the natural world around them. This interest, however, developed only slowly. Until well into the eighteenth century, Nature in the raw continued to inspire mistrust in the hearts of all civilised men and women. It might no longer have been necessary for gardeners to put her in a strait-jacket as in former days, insisting on the extreme artificiality of quincunxes, knot gardens or elaborate topiary mazes; none the less, to be properly acceptable she had to be disciplined or, as they liked to put it, 'educated' – in the manner exemplified by such painters as Poussin or Claude Lorrain, whose trees were always in full leaf, hills always verdant, streams always fresh and clear, irrigating a mild and smiling prospect exclusively peopled by gods and goddesses, nymphs and shepherds – the old Arcadian never-never land as preserved in those interminable three-volume novels so popular in the days of the *Roi Soleil*. Any attempt to depict the world as it was, as opposed to the world as it might have been – with peasant hovels and muddy puddles, dead branches and piles of manure – was greeted by polite *dilettanti* with a well-bred shudder and left with every show of relief to the Dutch, who were known to like that sort of thing.

Worst of all, it was generally agreed, were the Alps,which represented Nature at her most un-civilised, besides being the principal impediment to all those who contemplated an Italian journey. Horace Walpole, crossing them in 1739 with his friend the poet Thomas Gray, described the experience in a letter to his friend Richard West:

So, as the song says, we are in fair Italy! I wonder we are; for on the very highest precipice of Mount Cenis, the devil of a discord, in the similitude of sour wine, had got amongst our Alpine savages, and set them a-fighting with Gray and me in the chairs: they rushed him by me on a crag, where there was scarce room for a cloven foot. The least slip had tumbled us into such a fog, and such an eternity, as we should never have fought our way out of again. We were eight days in coming hither from Lyons; the four last crossing the Alps. Such uncouth rocks, and such uncomely inhabitants! My dear West, I hope I shall never see them again! At the foot of Mount Cenis we were obliged to quit our chaise, which was taken all to pieces and loaded on mules; and we were carried in low arm-chairs on poles, swathed in beaver bonnets, beaver stockings, muffs and bear-skins. When we came to the top, behold the snows fallen! and such quantities, and conducted by such heavy clouds that hung glouting, that I thought we could never have waded through them. The descent is two leagues, but steep and rough as O.'s father's face, over which, you know, the devil walked with hobnails in his shoes...

'Uncouth rocks': alas, poor Horace! For him – as, we may imagine, for most of his contemporaries – that was all the Alps had to offer. How differently, though, he would have reacted half a century later; for by then – the year of the French Revolution – man's whole outlook on the world about him had changed. Romanticism was in the air: he was no longer afraid to see Nature as an un-bridled force, himself as a leaf blown hither and thither by the wind. As for landscape, the days were past when it would be seen as nothing better than a backdrop for portraits, or dressed up in ridiculous Bo-Peep travesty; now, in its real rather than its idealised form, it was appreciated as it had never been before outside the Low Countries. New concepts were introduced to analyse it, new words coined or adapted to describe them. A pleasant and unthreatening view of valley and hill might be thought 'picturesque'; for the Alps, in the other hand, one word only would serve. They were, indisputably, 'sublime'.

And so, at long last, the land that lay beyond them was seen for what it was, and Italy stood revealed: not the pastoral Italy of Virgil and Horace, nor yet the political, strife-torn Italy of Dante, still less the sinister Italy, dark and vengeful, of Shakespeare, Webster or Le Tourneur; instead, the Italy that nature and her people had made her – a green and fertile land of astonishing variety, blessed with a gifted people and a benign climate; a land rich in history and ancient tradition and, moreover, one possessed of an unrivalled artistic and architectural heritage; a source of limitless interest and pleasure to all those with eyes to see and a mind to understand. As revelations go, we might have thought it a fairly obvious one; the only wonder is that it was so long in coming.

There was a travel poster in the nineteen-twenties and thirties that was probably more successful than any other in persuading people to travel to southern Europe. From somewhere in its bottom left-hand corner a long and luxurious train of Wagon-Lits was seen entering a tunnel. The industrial landscape that it was leaving in its wake was dark and gloomy, with swirls of fog and what looked like quite heavy rain falling from a steel-grey sky. Towards the upper right of the poster, the same train was emerging from the tunnel into a green and fertile valley, luscious with lemon trees and basking in what was obviously perpetual sunshine, while far away in the distance there shimmered a cobalt sea. The message could hardly be missed. *Kennst du das Land, wo die Zitronen blühn?* (Do you know the country where the lemons bloom?) Of course we knew it, even if we did not know our Goethe. The land was Italy, and it was all that we could do not to make straight for Victoria Station.

The photographs that you will find in the pages that follow are a good deal more subtle than the picture on the travel poster (even though on me at least they tend to have much the same effect); similarly, the title under which they have been collected has been chosen with care. 'The Italian Landscape', for example, would have been ridiculous: how could there possibly be any such thing? No country in Europe, surely, can boast such an astonishing range of climatic conditions and geological formations. There are parts of Italy which could easily be taken for England or France, Germany or Holland, Greece or even Norway. On the other hand, there is one sort of landscape at any rate which can instantaneously be recognised as Italian, through and through; and it may be worth trying briefly to identify it here.It is I believe, typically Tuscan. Not too flat, of course, but not mountainous either: just green, rolling hills, some of them quite steep, a few topped with little towns, each with its church and attendant *campanile*. In one of the valleys between there runs a winding river, crossed by an occasional hump-backed bridge. To each side of it, the fields are planted with olive and vine; others have been left for pasture, in which cattle or sheep can be added to according to taste. Here and there, apparently at random but in fact most carefully positioned, sometimes in lines, sometimes in clusters, but more often outlined all alone against the cloud-streaked sky, our eye falls on that most quintessential of Italian trees, the cypress. The picture is complete.

And, of course, a picture is exactly what it is – indeed, not so much one picture as thousands of them. For this view is familiar to us not just because we ourselves have seen it countless times when driving through Tuscany, but because it – or something like it – was the favourite background for the Tuscan, and indeed for almost all the Italian painters of the High Renaissance. To the Umbrians, too, it meant home; while the great Venetians, understandably reluctant to set their subjects against the flat featureless scenery of the lagoon, were accustomed to borrow that of the land lying a little further to the north and west – parts of which could easily be taken for Tuscany, and from which, incidentally, a surprising number of them had originally come. We see it, again and again, behind the Madonnas, saints and biblical scenes of Giovanni Bellini, of the Bassano family (who took their name from their birthplace), of Gian Battista Cima (who, as we are constantly reminded, hailed from nearby Conegliano) and of all their innumerable followers. Small wonder that for many of us that landscape was inescapably associated with Italy long before we ever crossed the channel.

But Tuscany has other landscapes too, with other artistic associations; and of these perhaps the strangest is that which we see portrayed in the works of Duccio, Simone Martini or any of the other Sienese painters of the early *trecento*. It is a stark, barren, sublunar world of bare, ash-coloured earth, pock-marked with caves and the occasional small heap of rocks, and slashed by sudden ravines: a world which provides the perfect setting for St Anthony and his demons or for St Simeon on his pillar but which, even when softened by the occasional tree – invariably topped by a blob of what appears to be green sponge, in the manner of those sometimes used to embellish architectural models – always seems to me a trifle harsh for the Nativity of the Miracles of St Francis. Until quite recently I took this landscape to be a simple matter of stylisation, something that no more aimed at an accurate representation than did the conventional signs on an Ordnance Survey map; then, just two or three years ago, I went on a walking tour in Tuscany and suddenly, some twenty or thirty miles south of Siena, found myself in that very country that I never thought to exist. Here were the caverns and the ravines, there on the bare hills the spongy little trees. If John the Baptist or St Anthony Abbot had suddenly emerged from behind the rocks I should hardly have raised an eyebrow.

But let us return for a moment to the Venetian lagoon. Have I, perhaps, been a little hard on it? Well, yes and no. Flat and featureless it unquestionably is; yet it too possesses its own ethereal beauty – a melancholy magic that, especially on grey autumnal evenings, can become almost tangible – and to me it has always been one of the eternal mysteries that it had so little attraction for the Venetian painters. Of them all, only Francesco Guardi ever seems to have done it anything like justice, and even he did not do so very often. As for the rest, the trouble was, I believe, that they were simply too Venetian. What they liked was colour and brilliance, luxury – the more opulent the better – and sumptuousness, crispness and clarity. The Grand Canal at noon on a spring morning – now *that* was a subject for anyone; the sandbanks beyond Murano, on the other hand, misty and bird-haunted, were a good deal less likely to appeal to the young English *milords* on the Grand Tour.

How much better, one feels, the Dutch would have handled it; how instinctively they would have responded to the challenge, capturing all the langour and the loneliness and the chill of the November dusk. Sadly, they preferred their own polders. Among the French, few of them would have been much good (with the possible exception of Watteau) until the coming of the impressionists, of whom one would have had high hopes; but in the event even they proved something of a disappointment. Monet, above all, could have done wonderful things, as he did on the Thames in London; but like the majority of his colleagues when they got to Venice at all – and a surprising number of them never made it – he was immediately seduced by the splendour of the city itself and paid all too little attention to the strange amphibious world that surrounded it and gave it its point and purpose. Besides, if the Venetians were too Venetian, the French impressionists were probably too French: few of them ever felt properly at home, or were able to give of their best, outside their native land. Indeed, of all the regiments of foreign artists who have flocked to Venice for the past five centuries and more, one painter, and one only seems to me to have caught the true spirit of its environment. That painter was J. M. W. Turner. But then, one might have guessed it: to quote Browning again, it's a subject made to his hand.

The Adriatic coast of Italy technically begins, I suppose, to the north and east of the Venetian lagoon – among the sand dunes and the shingle of that low-lying and rather desolate country around Grado and Quileia. Relatively few visitors to Venice drive out this far; but for those that do, the rewards are great.

Nowadays little more than villages, in ancient times each was the seat of a Patriarch – the incessant and furious quarrels between the two rival men of God lending much animation to the early chapters of Venetian history. Ultimately – though not a moment too soon, since for centuries it had caused nothing but trouble – the Patriarchate of Aqileia was brought firmly to an end; the Patriarchs of Grado moved down to the Rialto, changed their title accordingly and continue today, in a still unbroken line, as Patriarchs of Venice. But the two old cathedrals still stand – that of Aquileia going back to the fourth century and that of Grado to the sixth – and both have kept their glorious mosaic pavements as venerable as they are themselves. In particular, the representation of Jonah and the Whale in that of Aquileia lingers long in the memory.

Beyond Venice the same flat, marshy country continues, around and across the estuaries of the Adige and the Po, past the lovely old abbey of Pomposa and the lagoons and *lidi* of Comacchio, to Ravenna. It is, on the whole, an unsatisfactory landscape – and not only to the eye, since in former times it was notorious for the malaria which almost certainly caused the death of Dante in 1321: to this day it remains the last place I would recommend to convalescents. Nowadays even the sea itself has retreated from it – several miles since the days of Ravenna's sixth- and seventh-century greatness. The exquisite church of S. Apollinare in Classe, which is nowadays all that is left of its ancient port of Classis, now stands silent and alone amid the fields.

Perhaps it is these desolate and insalubrious surroundings that make the city so difficult to love. Venice is insulated by her lagoon; Ravenna, now land-locked, seems part and parcel of her landscape and somehow dragged down by it. How sad, I always feel, that the ancient seat of Byzantine power in Italy – and a city that still contains half a dozen of the greatest works of art in the whole country – should be permeated by an atmosphere so strangely oppressive. Our spirit soars when we come face to face with Justinian and Theodora, standing in all their splendour to each side of the high altar of San Vitale; or with St Lawrence, tripping lightly with his gridiron across the walls of Galla Placidia's tomb; or with the river god of the Jordan, lending so deliciously pagan a touch to the scene as he pops out of the water to watch the Baptism of Christ in the cupola of the Orthodox Baptistry: but the moment we are back in the street, down it comes again with a bump – and we long to be away.

South of Ravenna, we enter what is for me *terra incognita*. I have never been to Rimini, but the famous *Tempio Malatestiano* is largely a post-war restoration and all that I have heard of the modern town suggests that poor Francesca is probably a good deal better off being blown around the Inferno. As for Ancona and its surroundings, which I have visited only once, many years ago and at night, I have no recollection; it bears, I suspect, all too little resemblance to my mental picture of it, derived from Pinturicchio's picture in the Piccolomini Library of Siena Cathedral. Things may get better as we drive down to the Marches (where there is always the possibility of a quick trip up to Urbino) and on through the Abruzzi and Molise; but I do not expect really to cheer up until we reach Monte Gargano, that curious spur that juts out half-way down the calf of the Italian boot and marks a sudden qualitative change in the scenery of the Adriatic coast.

You see it coming from many miles away – a vast hump on the horizon, unexpected and a little threatening, looming up like a thundercloud. Then, as you approach and the road begins its climb, you slowly become conscious that it is not just the landscape that has changed: it is the whole spirit of the country around you. The very air seems full of noises; and you are not altogether surprised to learn that the Christian religion is stronger here – but also closer to the pagan – than anywhere else in Italy. Nor is there any more fertile breeding ground for local saints – the most remarkable of whom, in recent years, has been the celebrated Padre Pio.

It was some time in the early sixties, on my way down to Apulia to research my first book, that I found myself by chance in the little town of San Giovanni Rotundo and decided – for no other reason than that dusk was falling and I had been driving long enough – to stay there the night. When I walked into the hotel however I discovered that it was given over almost entirely to the pilgrim trade, standing as it did on the very doorstep of Padre Pio's monastery; and the first question I was asked at the reception desk was whether I wanted a wake-up call at half-past three to attend the early mass at which he always officiated. I cannot deny that there was a moment of hesitation: the following day threatened to be a long one, and I had no particular wish to make it longer still. When, on the other hand, would I have another opportunity to see at close quarters a man whose hands and feet were said to bear the stigmata and who was generally believed to be a living saint? Yes, I said, of course I would like a call; then I had the quickest and, as I remember, the nastiest of dinners – for religious enthusiasm and good cooking seldom, alas, go together – and retired to bed.

At ten minutes to four the next morning I joined the faithful outside the hideous monastery church – recently reconstructed in the style of a large municipal swimming-pool, to cope with the ever-increasing crowds. Their pent-up excitement was plain, as was the determination of each to be the first into the building the moment the doors opened; and indeed the young monk who opened them a few minutes later – and who had, I imagined, been chosen for his agility – had to leap back as he did so and flatten himself against the wall to avoid being trampled underfoot. Jaws set and elbows flailing, the pilgrims poured into the church, men and women separating into two streams and jostling themselves into positions as close as they could get to the altar – women to the north, men to the south. Scarcely were we all settled when Padre Pio walked in and the mass began.

His appearance came as no surprise; there were photographs galore of him all over the town. A big, burly peasant was what he looked like and what he was, with thin close-cropped grey hair, a scrubby beard and a tough, no-nonsense face; nothing overtly saintly, far less sanctimonious. The only thing that distinguished him, even faintly, from his fellows was a pair of small brown mittens which covered the palms of his hands – concealing, one assumed, the stigmata – and the rapt, even trance-like expression which remained, utterly unchanging, for the two hours and more that the mass continued.

When it was over there was another rush, this time into what might have been called a sacristry but which was essentially a long reception room in which the saint could receive his devotees. There must have been fifty or sixty of them that morning – some obviously dying, one or two half-witted, many with tears already streaming down their cheeks. As he walked down the lines, stopping for a moment or two with each, the rough, no-nonsense approach was more striking than ever; kneelers were roughly dragged to their feet; one snivelling child was told firmly to stiffen up, and given a smart clout over the ear for good measure. Then, quite suddenly, he was gone; and back we all went to the hotel for breakfast.

The mystery of Monte Gargano – a mystery of which Padre Pio is only one of the more recent manifestations – goes back to May 9, 493, when the Archangel Michael is said to have appeared to Bishop Laurentius of Siponto and to have left behind his great iron spur. Ever since that day, for nearly fifteen centuries, the cave in which the event occurred – it lies more or less underneath the town of Monte Sant' Angelo – has been a place of pilgrimage. You approach it from above, down a seemingly interminable winding staircase, its walls covered with votive offerings – arms and legs, hands and feet, hearts and stomachs and breasts, stamped out of time (or occasionally some less base metal) and left as permanent memorials to all those diseased or injured organs which have been restored to health and use thanks to the intervention of the Archangel. Interspersed among them are photographs of children in archangelic costume, resplendent in their tinfoil wings and biscuit-tin breastplates and brandishing wooden swords, as often as not accompanied by their own drawings of the accidents from which they have recovered – the trees from which they have fallen, the bulls that have gored them, the cars that have run them down. At last you emerge in the cave itself: dark and moss-encrusted, loud with the blessed mutter of prayer and the dripping of water from the roof, which is carefully collected by those in authority and distributed to the faithful in little plastic beakers. It was here, in the year 1016, that a party of young Norman pilgrims returning from the Holy Land were accosted by a Lombard patriot, who sought their help in liberating South Italy from Byzantine domination – an encounter which resulted in the invasion of the peninsula by the Normans and, half a century later, in their conquest of Sicily; but that is a story which I have told elsewhere and has no place in these pages.

It does, however, radically affect the scenery to the south; for the Gargano stops as abruptly as it begins, and beyond it lies Norman country: no longer mountainous nor yet flat and alluvial, but a land of rolling, tawny hills, some still crowned with the ruins of castles, sweeping gently down to a rougher, rockier coast and – since the Adriatic is already beginning to narrow – a choppier sea. And there, between the hills and coast, stretches the greatest glory of Apulia – the double chain of romanesque cathedrals that continues right down the peninsula: Barletta, Trani, Bisceglie, Mofetta, Giovinazzo, Ditono, Canosa (burial place of Count Bohemund of Antioch) and perhaps half a dozen others of equally stunning quality. The series reaches its climax with Bari – which, as well as its cathedral, boasts the even more splendid church of St Nicholas (Santa Claus if you prefer) whose body was brought by Bariot sailors from his tomb at Myra in Asia Minor and reburied here in the twelfth century. Nowhere in the *mezzogiorno* is there a greater church than this.

My own personal favourite, however, has always been the cathedral of Trani, the scene of one of the bravest modern architectural experiments I have ever come across. It stands isolated on its own little rocky peninsula, with the sea on three sides. Some time during the nineteen-fifties the building, like most of its fellows in the area, was shorn of the baroque accretions of more recent centuries and restored to its uncluttered romanesque; but at Trani that was not all. The superintendent of Monuments for Apulia – a man, clearly, of considerable imagination and no little courage – went further: he quite simply removed the outer wall from the entire bay opposite the altar to the north side, and replaced it with an enormous sheet of plate glass. Thanks to the inner buttresses, this glass is invisible from the greater part of the nave; its effect, however, is to flood the entire building with a brilliant marine light, bringing as it were the surrounding landscape – or seascape – right into the cathedral and making the building a part of its surroundings in a way that would have been impossible until relatively recent years. In theory, such an action was unforgivable and should never have been permitted; in practice, it has resulted in a *coup de théâtre* of such power that one can only applaud.

Away from the sea, the landscape of Apulia is wild but unspectacular, infused for me with the spirit of the most extraordinary of the Holy Roman Emperors: Frederick II, known in his youth as *puer Apuliae*, the Boy from Apulia, and later as *Stupor Mundi*, the Astonishment of the World. Grandson of Roger II, Norman King of Sicily and the most dazzling monarch of his day, and of the Emperor Frederick Barbarossa, he spent his early childhood at the court in Palermo – where he acquired his grounding in Greek and Arabic as well as in German, Italian, Latin and Norman French – before moving to Apulia which, despite a life spent almost constantly on the move, remained his favourite home. From his Sicilian grandfather he had inherited an insatiable curiosity about the natural and physical worlds, together with a passion for art and architecture, of both of which he was an enthusiastic patron; he travelled to Jerusalem and regained it from the Saracens by the sheer charm and power of his personality, without firing a shot; he gathered around him an intellectual and cultivated court in which, *inter alia*, the sonnet was invented; meanwhile in his spare time he wrote the first serious work on falconry, *De Arte Venandi cum Avibus*, which is still studied today. Embracing – as few men have ever done – the whole civilisation of western Europe, equally at home in both the Teutonic and Latin cultures, Frederick stands out head and shoulders above all his contemporaries; while his immense twelve-sided castle, known as Castel del Monte and recently restored after long years of deterioration and decay, still dominates the landscape he loved and seems to reflect his own many-faceted personality – that of the first and one of the greatest Renaissance princes, two hundred years before his time.

Apulia ends with two wonderful surprises: Lecce, one of the loveliest baroque towns in all Italy, and finally Otranto – the stress it should be remembered falls on the first syllable – only fifty kilmometres or so from S. Maria di Leuca, at the very tip of the Italian heel. My memory of it, after well over a quarter of a century, is that of a small and blindingly white little town set against a deep blue sea. The effect was, I remember thinking, almost Moorish; and indeed Otranto was conquered more than once by Saracens during the ninth and tenth centuries. For all that, its greatest glory is Christian; for on the floor of its Cathedral, in the twelfth century, the people of Otranto conceived the breathtaking plan of depicting in mosaic the entire history of the world, beginning with the Creation. The endearingly naive Romanesque of this pavement could hardly make more of a contrast with the Byzantine sophistication of Grado and Aquileia at the other end of the Adriatic; but each is in its own way a masterpiece and there can be few lengths of coastline anywhere that are enclosed within such superb parentheses.

Of Luciana – the instep of Italy – I know little beyond what I have read in Carlo Levi's *Christ Stopped at Eboli*, which hardly whets the appetite: bare chalky hills of dazzling whiteness, but desolate and desperately poor. Calabria too has generally had a bad press, except from that irresistible old reprobate Norman Douglas; but inland it can be wondrously beautiful and, in a few places, still almost unbelievably unspoilt, with olive trees the size of elms and occasionally – the village of Rossano in particular springs to mind – a ravishing little Byzantine church to remind us that this was a part of *magna Graecia* that remained under the sway of Constantinople right up to the late eleventh century. The same goes for the eastern coast of Calabria, off which in 1972, just opposite the little village of Riace Marina, a scuba-diver on holiday noticed, eight metres down, a bronze arm projecting from the sea bed. He told the local authorities, who immediately set off to investigate; and the result was the most exciting archaeological discovery since Tutankhamen: two life-size bronze figures, both masterpieces, one of them most probably the work of Phidias himself. They now occupy a room to themselves (apart from the regiments of squealing schoolchildren who nowadays turn every Italian gallery into a nightmare) in the Museum of Reggio di Calabria, and must, despite the children, on no account be missed.

At this point in our tour there is a strong temptation to cross the Straits of Messina and launch ourselves on Sicily (particularly as I happen to be writing these words in a hotel room just below Taormina). That temptation must, however, be resisted: Sicily is a world of its own, and deserves individual treatment later. And so, sparing little more than a passing nod from Scylla to Charybdis – or is it the other way round? To me they have always been the Rozencrantz and Guildenstern of classical geography – we leave the Straits of Messina behind us and head north-east

... mid shore-descending pines,
Where, blue as any peacock's neck, the Tyrrhene ocean shines.

Kipling was, of course, perfectly right: of Italy's two flanking seas, the Tyrrhenian is a considerable improvement on the Adriatic, deeper and darker – the mountains frequently sweeping straight down to the sea – and somehow healthier all round. In 1071 the Normans under Robert Guiscard – the greatest and most successful military adventurer between Julius Caesar and Napoleon – captured Bari and drove the Greeks out of the peninsula once and for all; but I am told that a few remote villages remained after the second world war in which a debased form of Greek – one of its hallmarks, apparently, being the substitution of 'ps' – the Greek letter *psi* – by 'sp', making 'fish' *spara*, and bread *spomi* – was still spoken.

16

For all its beauty, however, there can be no doubt that Calabria remains, to the curious traveller, just a little bit dull. Things get a lot more exciting when we reach Campania and suddenly see ahead of us, only a few hundred yards away from the water's edge, the Doric temples of Paestum. Few ancient Greek buildings anywhere are older than the ridiculously-named Basilica (which was in fact dedicated to Hera); few are in a better state of preservation; none are more moving. Then, once we are round the Gulf of Salerno, comes Italian scenery at its most spectacular: Amalfi, the Sorrento peninsula and Capri, with the shadow of Ischia to the north-west across the Bay of Naples and the plume of Vesuvius rising into the blue. It is, inevitably, the Italy of a thousand chocolate boxes, a million calendars, a billion post cards; but it is none the worse for that, and I know of no one whose heart will not beat a little faster at the sight.

Our hearts will, alas, slow down all too soon as we approach Naples, that perennial ulcer on the shin of Italy that has proved impervious to every treatment, every remedy. We shall be well advised to pass on as quickly as we can, ignoring the huge and hideous Bourbon palace at Caserta (gloomiest in Europe, excepting only the Vienna Hofburg) but, I hope, making a brief detour to Capua for the sake of Frederick II, who held his court there. The ancient town barely survived an appalling battering during the last war; but the site, commanding a great loop of the Volturno, is superb – and the Museum still has wonderful things. Nor can we possibly miss the little romanesque church in the neighbouring village of St Angelo in Formis, where the frescos still blaze almost as brilliantly as they did on the day they were painted, some nine centuries ago

The great mother-monastery of Monte Cassino suffered even greater devastation than Capua, and in the same month: by the time the war had passed it by, there was scarcely one stone left on another. The monks remained, however: they had after all been there since the sixth century, when their Order had been founded by St Benedict himself, and – though their monastery has since been destroyed no less than five times – they are there to this day: if you raise your eyes half-way up the hillside to your right as you hurtle towards Rome, you may sometimes see them, their black habits hitched up and tucked into their belts, tilling their fields as they always have, for all the world like some illustration in a medieval psalter or Book of Hours.

Now we are entering Lazio, and with it the Roman *Campagna* – a moment signalled by the appearance in strength of that most evocative of trees, which is to Rome what the cypress is to Florence: the umbrella pine. Soon, too, we come upon other indications more unmistakable still: a broken statue, an ancient shrine, a fallen column, a stretch of aqueduct. This above all is the landscape of the Grand Tour, painted with unending enthusiasm and every degree of accomplishment and success, in oil and water-colour, by artists amateur and professional, from every corner of Europe and America, time and time again. As such, it belongs firmly to the eighteenth and nineteenth centuries, while the traditional Tuscan landscape described at the beginning of this essay is essentially a fifteenth- and sixteenth-century one. Would that our own century could claim it too; alas, it is rapidly being swallowed up in the ever-advancing industrial sprawl, and by the year 2000 – baring some miracle of conservation of which there is precious little sign as yet – it may well have ceased to exist altogether. We must enjoy it while we can.

Fortunately, the Roman Campagna and the Lazio can also provide us with another, very different sort of landscape: more artificial perhaps, but protected and consequently enjoying, with any luck, a longer expectancy of life. For here, with Tuscany, is the home of the great Renaissance garden – that endlessly fascinating combination of nature, architecture and sculpture that sixteenth-century and seventeenth-century Italy made its own. Even in Rome itself there are several – those, for example, of the Villa Borghese, or of the Villa Medici (now the French Academy) on the Pincian, or of the Villa Pamphili, or even of the Vatican; and within an hour or two's drive you will find countless more – those of the Villa d'Este at Tivoli, of the Villas Aldobrandini and Torlonia at Frascati, of the Villa Farnese at Caprarola, of the Villa Lante at Bagnaia. Strangest of all are the gardens of the Villa Orsini at Bomarzo, designed around a whole cluster of rocky outcrops out of which were carved huge giants and monsters of the most alarming kind. Bomarzo may have little to do with the Renaissance as we normally understand the term; but I know of few places that offer a more rewarding site for a picnic in the heat of a Roman summer.

North of Rome we enter Etruscan country; then, if we stay fairly near the coast, we find ourselves gradually descending into the green flatlands that form the valley of the Arno and, beginning immediately to the west of Florence, broaden steadily towards Pisa and the sea. How much more sensible, then, to stick to the hills as long as possible – nearly always a sound principle in Italy; to follow the young Tiber up to Perugia and the unbelievably blue Lake Tarismeno, then to continue through the Apennines through Arezzo and Bibbiena (not forgetting the enchanting little hill-top town of Poppi) into the Mugello, the upper basin of the Sieve, where Tuscany is at its most Tuscan and they make the finest wine in the whole country. After that, unfortunately, the hills can no longer be stuck to unless we are on foot; there is no road along the crest of the northern Apennines, and we consequently have no choice but to skirt them, either along that unusually boring inland road that leads straight as a die north-west across Italy from Rimini to Piacenza, or along the narrow coastal strip where the motorway is composed entirely of alternating viaducts and tunnels and the old road is one interminable ribbon development all the way round the Gulf of Genoa to the French border. The former, while offering the by no means negligible consolations of Bologna (one of my favourite Italian cities), Reggio Emilia (where the art gallery contains a most remarkable picture of the abdication of our King Charles I) and Parma (where you may have the pleasure of staying in Italy's most charmingly named hotel, the Grande Albergo Button), is scenically a non-starter; the latter, on the other hand, enables you to make a brief and memorable detour to the one minute enclave that remains relatively unspoilt, the *Cinque Terre*. Until a few years ago the sole link between these five little fishing villages and the outside world was a network of tortuous mountain paths. Now, inevitably, there is a road; but recent visitors assure me that the *Cinque Terre* have managed so far to preserve much of their character, and with any luck they may continue to do so for a few more years yet.

The greatest landscape in Genoa is that of its cemetery. More rewarding than even Highgate or Père Lachaise, its marbles and mausoleums climb up a steep hillside above the Bisagno valley to the north-west of the city in a riot of funerary sculpture that tells us more than any art gallery ever could about Genoese life in the late nineteenth and early twentieth century in a whole series of affecting *tableaux*;

here Papa lies on his deathbed, immaculately dressed in his morning coat, every stitch of his socks, every buttonhole of his waistcoat faithfully delineated, while Mama, hand over eyes, weeps silently at his feet and the children in their sailor suits kneel in a mournful row along the side. There stands the old lady who sold peanuts in the Piazza Acquaverde for fifty years and put all her savings into a life-size statue of herself and her wares, every peanut an individual work of art.

Once through Genoa, there is little temptation to hug the coast any longer; if we can, however, we should stick it out as far as Savona before turning with relief up into the mountains again to Turin – the least visited and consequently most underestimated of all the great Italian cities – and thence north through the Val d'Aosta to what must always be, with the Sorrento peninsula, the most breathtakingly magnificent scenery of all: that of the high Alps. Which is where, with Horace Walpole, we came in.

'Italy without Sicily is inconceivable,' wrote Goethe in 1787, 'here is the key to it all.' Alas, Goethe was neither the first genius nor the last to talk nonsense. Sicily can claim – though she would not be particularly proud to do so – a certain amount of shared history with Naples and South Italy, but her first connection with the North came only with the Risorgimento; she does not explain Italy any more than Italy explains her, the two have always been separate entities. One might imagine that the Straits of Messina, like the English Channel, were a relatively recent creation, and that a few thousand years ago Italy and Sicily formed a single land mass in much the same way as did England and continental Europe; but one would be wrong. The Straits, nowadays only a couple of miles across, were once a good deal wider, and have in fact narrowed over the millennia. Sicily remains what she always was, a being apart.

Her tragedy, too, has always been the same: the tragedy, as I wrote twenty-five years ago in another connection, of a beautiful woman who has been raped too often and been betrayed too often and is no longer fit for love or marriage. Thanks to her superbly strategic position, her two outstanding natural harbours at Palermo and Syracuse, the fertility of her soil and the perpetual benediction of her climate, she has been fought over and occupied in turn by all the great powers that have at various times striven to extend their sway over the Mediterranean: Phoenicians, Greeks, Carthaginians, Romans, Goths, Byzant-ines, Arabs, Normans, Germans, Spaniards, French and finally, the Italians themselves. And all, in one way or another, for good or for ill, have left their mark.

Nature, however, elsewhere so lavish with her blessings, also inflicted upon Sicily a curse: Etna. Highest, angriest and potentially the most lethal of European volcanoes, rising in a long, unbroken and deceptively gentle slope to a point nearly eleven thousand feet above the sea, it has burst out in more than thirty major eruptions over the last two hundred years. Even in its quiet moments, it never sleeps: every night from the coast road that runs from Catania to Messina – and from certain of the more expensive hotel rooms in Taormina – you may see its crater glowing red against the night sky, periodically brightening, then fading, then brightening again as if some fairy-tale giant were drawing on a huge cigar. Around the base of the mountain, on the other hand, all is greenness and fertility.

But then Sicily is, as it has always been, a land of contrasts. Parts of it are intensely cultivated, with lush fields of corn, endless rows of vines and vast, carefully-tended groves of olive and citrus – the lemon trees at certain times of the year being so covered with fruit as to make them more yellow than green. Then you turn a corner: from one moment to the next, you are back in the wild, bare hills again, in a landscape unchanged since the days of the earliest inhabitants of the island. As you approach its heart, the mountains grow higher, the towns seemingly clinging ever more tightly to their sides; but in whatever direction you go it will never be too long before another bend in the road will suddenly reveal, far below you and quite startlingly blue, the distant sea. No wonder, one feels, that Sicily was the setting for so many of the myths of Ancient Greece. Everybody knows that the delightful fresh water spring down by the seashore in Syracuse is in reality the nymph Arethusa, transformed while escaping the clutches of Alphaeus the river-god; and all over the island you will find rivers and streams, mountains and hills of which, for well over two thousand years, similar tales have been told. The most fateful abduction in all mythology took place at Lake Pergusa, a distinctly sinister expanse of brackish water a few miles to the south of Enna; for this was the reputed entrance to the infernal regions, what Milton called

> that faire field
> of *Enna*, where Proserpin gathring flours
> Her self a fairer Floure by gloomie *Dis*
> Was gatherd, which cost *Ceres* all that pain
> To seek her through the World.

Had Ceres not found her daughter, the poor girl would have been doomed to spend all eternity in the Plutonic pit and we ourselves condemned to perpetual winter. Fortunately, it will be remembered, the goddess was able to come to an arrangement with the abductor, who agreed to release her for six months a year and thereby ensured our changing seasons.

So momentous an event, the effects of which continue to govern all our lives, would – one might have thought – have been enough to ensure that Lake Pergusa would have been respected. Alas, it has not. The Blue Guide to Sicily regretfully informs us that 'Its vegetation and birdlife have been virtually destroyed since the 1950s by the incongruous motor racing track which encircles it and other new buildings ... Its polluted waters are now drying up.' Nor is this the only desecration of post-war years. The strange propensity of Sicilian engineers to raise their new *autostrade* on arches for mile after mile – thus effectively building viaducts rather than roads – has had a disastrous effect on much of the landscape; while two stretches of coast in particular – those within range of the oil ports of Gela (where Aeschylus died, felled by a plummeting tortoise which a passing eagle had dropped on his bald head, under the mistaken impression that it was a rock) and Augusta, just south of Catania – have been the subject of public scandal.

We can only be thankful that so much of the island has, at least so far, been spared. The distant prospect of Segesta – which enjoys the loveliest setting of any Greek temple anywhere – had a narrow escape from the motorway but mercifully remains unscathed, and those driving from Palermo can still enjoy the memorable triple-tiered view of Cefalù – the huge shoulder of rock towering above, then the Norman cathedral, and finally the old town clustered close at its foot and sweeping down to the sea. And, while we are on the subject of Cefalù, let no traveller fail to enter that cathedral where, if he lifts his eyes to the high eastern apse, he will catch his breath in amazement – for there, gazing down at him from the conch with eyes that seem to penetrate to his very soul, is the tremendous mosaic of Christ Pantocrater with which the Norman King Roger II endowed the building in 1184, and which I have always believed to be the greatest portrait of the Redeemer in all Christian art.

If no other Norman monuments existed in Sicily save this one transcendent masterpiece, it would be enough to mark King Roger's reign as the island's golden age, a time when its people were probably happier than at any other period in their history. When his father and uncle had crossed the straits at the head of a small invading army in 1061, capturing Palermo eleven years later, they had found themselves confronted with two very different communities – a large Greek population which had already been there for nearly two thousand years and three flourishing Muslim emirates, formed after the Arab invasions some two hundred years before. Neither then nor afterwards, however, were the Normans numerous enough to rule the country on their own. Their only course was to enlist the support of those they had conquered, and it is this extraordinary combination of Latin, Greek, and Arab that gives Norman Sicily its unique fascination. To see it at its most dazzling you have only to go to the Palatine Chapel in the Royal Palace at Palermo. The ground plan is entirely western: a central nave, two flanking aisles, a few steps leading up to the chancel. But the walls are covered with Byzantine mosaics as fine as anything to be found in Constantinople, while the painted wooden stalactite roof is of the purest Arab workmanship – something that would do credit to Cairo, Cordova or Damascus. And this, remember, was the twelfth century – a time when everywhere else they were all at each other's throats, with the eastern and western Churches exchanging abuse and anathemas, Christians and Muslims slaughtering each other in the Crusades. Only here, in this one little island in the dead centre of the Mediterranean, did the three great civilisations live together in harmony and concord. It is not often in her sad history that Sicily has been given a chance to set an example; all the more reason never to forget that, for a few short decades in the middle ages it was a lesson to us all.

The twentieth century has been a hard one for landscape. Of all those that we have seen in this whirlwind tour of Italy, two only – the high Alps and the Renaissance gardens – have escaped defilement. (Or almost escaped it, since even there we cannot avoid the occasional ski lift or a glimpse of the municipal car park through the cypresses.) Of the once-glorious coastline that lies between La Spezia and Mentone I have already spoken. The Venetian lagoon must contend with the unlovely profile of Mestre and Marghera on the western horizon and the *motoscafi* ploughing their way through to Marco Polo airport in the north; the Sorrento peninsula is powdered with a dense dandruff of holiday villas; there are parts of Tuscany in which every little valley conceals its own individual factory, and others where the very concept of the village seems to have been abandoned – every new house being built two or three hundred yards from its nearest neighbours to the point where the eye cannot find a single expanse of unbroken green on which to rest. To compare a picture of the Bay of Naples painted only a hundred years ago with the same view today is little short of heart-breaking. And this inexorable process is not over; indeed, it probably never will be, until the entire country has been swallowed up by mindless development and the Italian countryside as we know it exists no more.

The danger, as we are all only too aware, is not confined to Italy. There are, however, few countries in western Europe in which rural development is more loosely controlled and the landscape more poorly protected. Recent legislation providing for the establishment of National Parks may do some good in certain extremely limited areas – the only one so far in existence is confined to the slopes of Mount Etna – but even that is no substitute for the general tightening-up of planning laws that the Italians so desperately need.

But there – this is not place to start beating the conservationist drum; and in any case you will find little enough evidence of landscape destruction in these ravishing photographs, all of which radiate that extraordinary quality of timelessness that Charlie Waite manages to capture like no other photographer I know. Seldom in his work will you catch sight of a human being. Buildings there are in plenty, but whether they are churches or ruined castles, farmhouses or barns or even whole villages, all of them seem to have grown organically out of the soil, to have merged into the surrounding landscape and become an integral part of it; never does he allow them to dominate or intrude.

How he achieves these miracles I cannot begin to understand. He himself has confirmed what should in fact be obvious enough – that he is not one of those photographers who clicks away endlessly exposing dozens of rolls of film a day. He searches – few of his vantage points, I suspect, are within miles of a road – watches, selects, composes, sets up his tripod – and then settles down to wait. Thus a single photograph can represent hours of walking – followed as likely as not by as many hours again of patient vigil, praying for that magic instant (which may easily never come) when the sun's angle, and the quality of the light that it sheds, enables him to freeze a fleeting picture into a permanent work of art. It must be lonely work, too: he tells me that he always travels alone, for how could he possibly ask anyone else to stand for hours on a freezing hilltop for a photograph that may quite possibly never be taken? And just imagine the disappointments: an ill-timed shower of rain; a suddenly rising mist; the cloud that obscures the sun at the critical moment; the concrete factory, hitherto unsuspected, that suddenly reveals itself after a back-breaking climb of hill or mountain, effectively turning a potential masterpiece into a might-have-been. A thoughtlessly parked car, even a passing lorry, could be enough to destroy a whole day's hard labour.

But then again, how deeply satisfying the successes – the occasions when the alchemy works and all the necessary elements come together exactly as they were meant to do. The lorry moves away; the passing aeroplane flies out of frame; the cloud clears; and the slanting sun catches the clump of trees exactly as it was meant to do. Then, and then only, the camera clicks; and those long, cold hours of waiting (never, one feels, has an artist been more appropriately named) are triumphantly vindicated. One photograph has been taken. In this book there are one hundred and forty-five of them.

Charlie Waite, it need hardly be said, would not want you to think about any of this. *Ars est celare artem*; the whole thing must be made to look effortless – something that any of us could do. He is no exhibitionist photographer; on the contrary, his pictures are almost always deliberately understated. It is only when we look at them carefully – and think about them – that we realise that nothing, absolutely nothing, has been left to chance. His object is simply to celebrate Italy: not the splendour of her towns and cities (as a thousand other photographic collections have done before) but the quiet serenity of her countryside and landscape. And even there, he does not try to dazzle us with three-star *vaut-le-détour* panoramas – none of the views in the following pages, I feel perfectly sure, has ever been the subject of a postcard – but simply to reveal the half-hidden beauty that lies everywhere in that most magical of countries, but which most of us take for granted, or are too blind or blasé to see. If we give his work the attention it deserves, our eyes will be opened and our visual perception increased a hundredfold. And that will be his – and our – reward.

John Julius Norwich
Giardini-Naxos, April 1989

TUSCANY

ITALIAN LANDSCAPES

SOUTH OF CERTALDO, TUSCANY

NORTH WEST OF SINALUNGA, TUSCANY

EAST OF GREVI IN CHIANTI, TUSCANY

WEST OF ASCIANO, TUSCANY

EAST OF AGIRA, SICILY

ORANGE TREE, SICILY

EAST OF MONTALCINO, TUSCANY

EAST OF SAN GIMIGNANO, TUSCANY

NORTH OF RAFALDI, NEAR AGRIGENTO, SICILY

NORTH OF RAFALDI, NEAR AGRIGENTO, SICILY

NEAR MONTEPULCIANO, TUSCANY

SOUTH OF MONTEPULCIANO, TUSCANY

EAST OF ASCIANO, TUSCANY

NORTH WEST OF AGRIGENTO, SICILY

PIERLE, NORTH OF UMBERTIDE, TUSCANY

ISNELLO, SOUTH OF CEFALU, SICILY

REGALBUTO, NORTH WEST OF CATANIA, SICILY

ROFRANO, NORTH WEST OF CAPRI, CAMPANIA

CASTIGLOINE DI SICILIA, SICILY

CULINGA, SOUTH OF LAMEZIA TERME, CALABRIA

PITIGLIANO, EAST OF GROSSETO, TUSCANY

BRIENZA, SOUTH WEST OF POTENZA, BASILICATA

MORANO CALABRO, NORTH OF CASTROVILLARI, CALABRIA

SAN GIMIGNANO, TUSCANY

NORTH OF MONTEVARCHI, TUSCANY

WEST OF SINALUNGA, TUSCANY

WEST OF TREQUANDA, TUSCANY

WEST OF SINALUNGA, TUSCANY

NORTH OF ASCIANO, TUSCANY

SOUTH OF PIENZA, TUSCANY

NORTH OF SAN GIOVANNI D'ASSO, TUSCANY

NORTH OF ARCIDOSSO, TUSCANY

EAST OF POGGIBONSI, TUSCANY

NEAR MONTALCINO, SOUTH OF SIENA, TUSCANY

NEAR VOLTERRA, TUSCANY

FONTAVIGNONE, SOUTH OF L'AQUILA, ABRUZZI

LAGO DE SALTO, WEST OF L'AQUILA, BORDER OF LATIUM AND ABRUZZI

VALLE DI CADORE, SOUTH OF CORTINA. D'AMPEZZO, DOLOMITES

S. IONA, ABOVE CELANO, ABRUZZI

CAPRADOSS0, SOUTH EAST OF RIETI, BORDER OF LATIUM AND ABRUZZI

TRESIVIO, EAST OF SONDRIO, LOMBARDY

SOUTH OF SIENA, TUSCANY

NEAR CANELA, SOUTH OF FOGGIA, APULIA

ASSISI, SOUTH EAST OF PERUGIA, UMBRIA

CASTEL DEL MONTE, SOUTH OF TERAMO, ABRUZZI

VAL D'AMPOLA, LOMBARDY

PASSO PORDOI, EAST OF BOLZANO, DOLOMITES

NORTH OF L'AQUILA, ABRUZZI

NEAR COLFIORITO, NORTH EAST OF FOLIGNO, UMBRIA

SIRMIONE, LOMBARDY

NEAR CASENOVE, WEST OF COLFIORITO, UMBRIA

SOUTH OF SIENA, TUSCANY

NEAR CASTELLINI IN CHIANTI, TUSCANY

CORTONA, TUSCANY

BASILICA SAN FRANCESCO, ASSISI, UMBRIA

NEAR BRESCIA, LOMBARDY

NORTH WEST OF SINALUNGA, TUSCANY

MARINA DI ALBRESE, SOUTH OF GROSSETO, TUSCANY

SOUTH OF LIVORNO, TUSCANY

NORTH OF TODI, UMBRIA

SOUTH OF DICOMANO, NORTH WEST OF FLORENCE, TUSCANY

NEAR SAN MARTINO, DOLOMITES

ABOVE BRUNICO, NORTH WEST OF DOLOMITES

LAGO DI BRAIES, NORTH OF CORTINA, DOLOMITES

LAGO DI MISURINA, NORTH OF CORTINA, DOLOMITES

PALE, NORTH WEST OF FOLIGNO, UMBRIA

SOUTH OF ROVERTO, NORTH WEST OF VICENZA, VENETO

SOUTH OF SIENA, TUSCANY

SANTA MARIA DEGLI ANGELI, SOUTH OF ASSISI, UMBRIA

WEST OF CELANO, ABRUZZI

NEAR CALTAGIRONE, NORTH EAST OF GELA, SICILY

CORTONA, TUSCANY

SAN ANTINO, SOUTH OF MONTALCINO, TUSCANY

NORTH OF SUBIACO, LATIUM

EAST OF RANDAZO, BELOW MOUNT ETNA, SICILY

NEAR MONTE SAN SAVINO, TUSCANY

NEAR MONTE OLIVETTO, NEAR ASCIANO, TUSCANY

SAN GIMIGNANELLO, EAST OF ASCIANO, TUSCANY

NORTH OF ROSARNO, CALABRIA

NEAR MONTE SAVINO, SOUTH OF SIENA, TUSCANY

SOUTH OF RADDA IN CHIANTI, TUSCANY

NORTH OF ROCARASO, ABRUZZI

NORTH OF LICENZE, LATIUM

PESCAGLIA, WEST OF BORGO A MOZZANO, TUSCANY

NORTH OF BISIGNANO, CALABRIA, SICILY

SOUTH OF SLAMONA, ABRUZZI

NORTH OF URBINO, MARCHES

NEAR LAKE COMO, LOMBARDY

ABOVE REGGIO DI CALABRIA

EAST OF AVELINO, CAMPANIA

WEST OF CASTELBUONO, NEAR CEFALU, SICILY

NORTH WEST OF COLL DI VAL D'ELSA, TUSCANY

NEAR SAN MARTINO IN GRANIA, SOUTH OF SIENA, TUSCANY

NEAR ASCIANO, TUSCANY

TUSCANY

NEAR MANTUA, LOMBARDY

NEAR BETTONA, SOUTH EAST OF PERUGIA, UMBRIA

NEAR COLLAZZONE, EAST OF MARSCIANO, UMBRIA

ABRUZZI

SOUTH OF TRIPONZO, UMBRIA

WEST OF CASCIA, UMBRIA

NEAR CASCIA, UMBRIA

NEAR SPOLETO, UMBRIA

WEST OF RIMINI, EMILIA-ROMAGNA

EAST OF RIETI, LATIUM

NEAR SAN GIMIGNANO

EAST OF SINALUNGA, TUSCANY

WEST OF REGALBUTO, SICILY

NEAR ASCIANO, SICILY

LAKE BLOSENA, LATIUM

SOUTH OF CASTEL NUOVA DI GARF, TUSCANY

NORTH OF SERRADIFLACO, WEST OF CALTANISSETTA, SICILY

CALABRIA

WEST OF TAURIANOVA, CALABRIA

SOUTH OF SIENA, TUSCANY

EAST OF MONTERANI D'ARBIA, TUSCANY

NORTH OF MENSANO, TUSCANY

WEST OF CORONA, DOLOMITES

MONTEROSSO ALMO, NORTH OF RAGUSA, SICILY

NEAR LONGARONE, SOUTH OF CORTINA, DOLOMITES

MOUNT ETNA FROM ROVITELLO, SICILY

NORTH OF FIRENZUOLO, EMILIA-ROMAGNA

WEST OF AREZZO, TUSCANY

WEST OF ASCIANO, TUSCANY

NEAR TIRIOLO, WEST OF CATANZARO, CALABRIA

EAST OF VITERBO, LATIUM

EAST OF MONTARNI D'ARBIA, TUSCANY

SOUTH OF CASOLE D'ELSA, TUSCANY

EAST OF STEFANO, SICILY

PIZZO, SOUTH OF LAMEZIA TERME, CALABRIA

LEONFORTE, NORTH EAST OF ENNA, SICILY

WEST OF CALTABELLOTTA, SICILY

WEST OF SAN ARCANGELO, BASILICATA

EAST OF L'AQUILA, ABRUZZI